Full of BALONEY!

Wacky, Happy Poetry

**Written and Illustrated
by
Jo Hudson**

Dedicated to those who imagine.

*"A special thanks to Terri for working her
T-crossing, I-dotting magic!"*

www.JoHudsonAuthor.com

This Book is for You IF ...

You love to giggle
Until your eyelashes wiggle
And your whole demeanor distorts.

Until your belly splits
And your nostrils spit
Bubbles and flubbles and snorts.

But if you don't like funny,
Would rather feel crummy,
ABORT! ABORT! ABORT!

Full of Baloney

Scuttlebutt had it that Newton Mahoney,
The kid who did news, was full of baloney.
The stories he told, the tales up his sleeve,
Were kooky and odd, sometimes hard to believe.

Newton Mahoney, a curious type,
Reported on things that didn't seem right.
He hunted for stories he knew would amuse
Then wrote them all up in his paper, Newt's News.

Newton was careful to always disclose
In each Newt's News printed edition,
That names and faces had all been changed,
Not disclosed without subject's permission.

Squeeze Those Knees!

Keep a tight squeeze
With your knuckles
And knees
On that trapeze

And if you sneeze,
Due to bad
Allergies,
Do NOT release!

MO͡USE

"If I were only a moose,"
Mouse thoughtfully deduced,
"I'd wear my antlers proudly.
I could squeak so LOUDLY!
It wouldn't be that hard to do.
Just put in an "O" and take out the "U.""

Hot Potato, Couch Potato, Spud

Hot Potato, Couch Potato, and Spud
Were brothers with varied ambitions.
The one objective they shared
Was a collective decision
To avoid, at all costs, the kitchen.

The Newitwoodents

The Newitwoodents knew it wouldn't,
So planted seeds of doubt.
But someone always came behind
And pulled the seed pods out.

The Newitwoodents plotted
To catch the sneaky thief
And soon nabbed Optum S. Tick,
Who laughed in disbelief.

"Why is your glass always full?"
His captors asked of Optum.
"It's not always full," he said,
"Just empty on the bottom."

Pea's Podcast

Pea's daily podcast
Was a popular broadcast
Among the local vegetation.

Potatoes baked twice,
Produce seeking advice,
Regularly tuned in to her station.

Eggplant's confused rant,
"Am I egg? Am I plant?"
Was the segment that went most viral.

A carrot who chose
To be more than a nose
Turned him into a national idol.

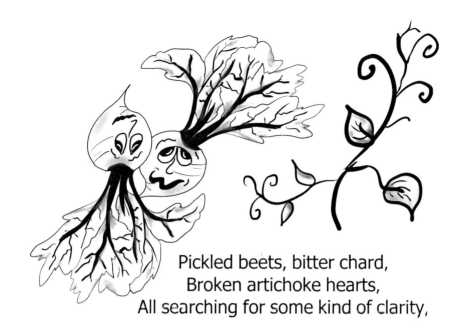

Pickled beets, bitter chard,
Broken artichoke hearts,
All searching for some kind of clarity,

Followed podcaster Pea
Partly because she
Cost less than traditional therapy.

Juggle Struggle!

I threw a ball
Up in the air,
Then two,
Then three,
Then four.

I couldn't stop.
I didn't dare.
More!
More!
More!

Colored balls
Filled the sky.
They seemed
to float
and hover.

But when they
Dropped,
I knew that I
Had better
Run for cover!

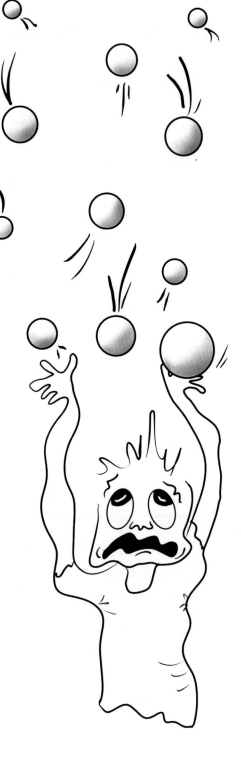

Hey, Riddle Riddle

Hey, Riddle Riddle
That's you in the middle.
Me I never see.

There's your style,
Your bright, toothy smile,
I see what you see.

Reflect a minute.
Put your best in it.
See you and you see me.

Unscramble me
And who I am
You will clearly see.

R

M

Bubble Burps

I felt the bubbles
Start to stir,
Rumble, tumble,
Pivot, whir!

They grew and grew,
Flopped and floated,
Turned and churned.
I was bloated!

There was no place
For me to hide.
The bubbles
Had to stay inside!

I was afraid
I might not squelch
The noise you make
When you belch.

I plugged my nose
And shut my mouth.
The bubbles seemed
To travel south.

Then a WHUMP!
A FLUMP! A LURCH!
And to my dismay,
My bottom burped!

The Dawdlers

Dilly, Dally, Tinker, and Doodle's
Efforts to achieve were futile.
All they accomplished,
All they ever got done,
Was to dilly, dally, tinker, and doodle.

Avian Eatery

On the corner of 7th and Pine,
Where birds and waterfowl dine,
Pelicans in the kitchen
Scoop soup and wash dishes
To ready the meal for the night.

Tables are set by a loon.
A trumpeter swan drops a spoon.
The waiters are geese,
Bows tied under their beaks,
And a sparrow warbles a tune.

An ostrich directs the crowd
That lines up to the edge of town.
She checks the bird roster,
Watching out for imposters,
As it's strictly no cats allowed.

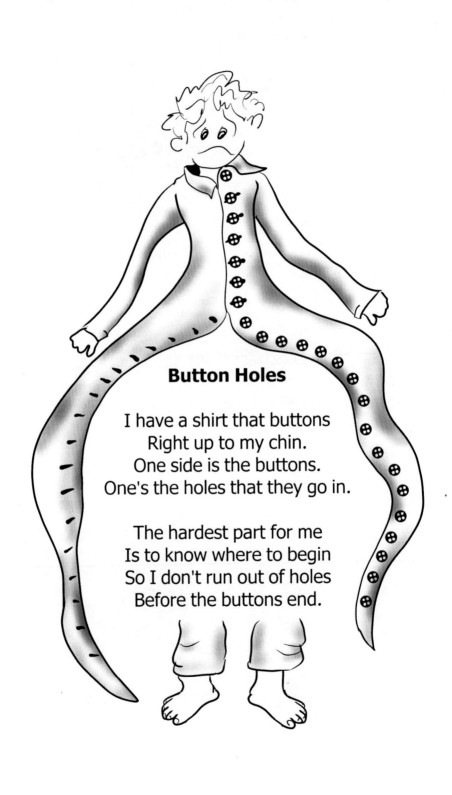

Button Holes

I have a shirt that buttons
Right up to my chin.
One side is the buttons.
One's the holes that they go in.

The hardest part for me
Is to know where to begin
So I don't run out of holes
Before the buttons end.

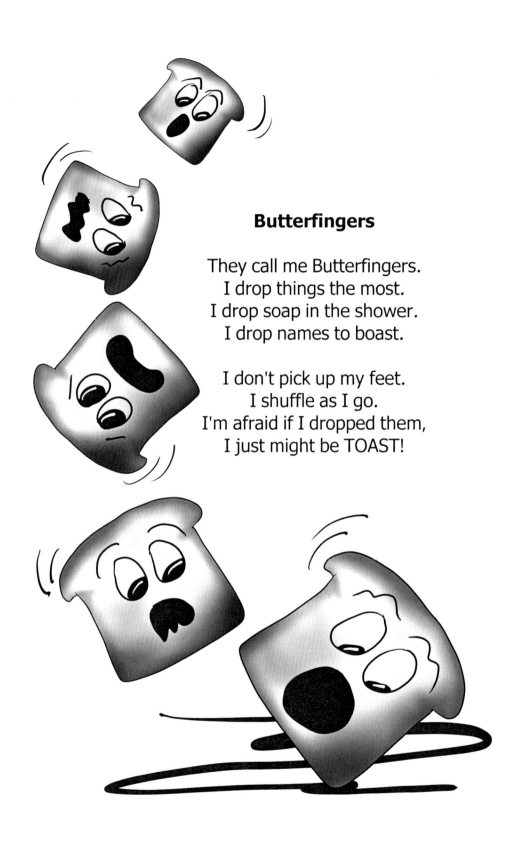

Butterfingers

They call me Butterfingers.
I drop things the most.
I drop soap in the shower.
I drop names to boast.

I don't pick up my feet.
I shuffle as I go.
I'm afraid if I dropped them,
I just might be TOAST!

The Great Freckle Fiasco

Freddie wished his freckles would all fall off his face.
He found them in the morning on his pillowcase.

His nose without his freckles tickled, so he sneezed.
The freckles got caught up in the resulting breeze.

Dropped by the breeze, freckles scattered on the floor,
Got swept up, thrown away, and taken out the door.

The trash that they were in was moved out to the curb,
Where it got knocked over by a cat chasing a bird.

They landed in a puddle and got stepped on by some feet,
Who drug them all along the muddy, messy street.

The feet, not knowing they had freckles on their toes,
Wiped them on the grass, where they were sprayed by a hose.

The water from the hose got mixed up with the rain
And washed the frightened freckles down the city drain.

Freddie tried to find his freckles
So he could be himself.
But they had disappeared.
He felt like someone else.

The freckles, also lonely with no face to call their own,
Made their way back up the drain to try to get back home.

They clung to red galoshes that were passing by,
Fell off on a sidewalk, more than grateful for the ride.

A familiar walkway, the freckles knew the place.
Inside a nearby house, they spotted Freddie's face.

The face did not look happy without them splattered on it.
The freckles were determined to take their place upon it.

They snuck into the house in an overnight intrusion,
And at daybreak they engaged in a freckle-face reunion.

Mr. B's POV

From Mr. B's point of view,

Everything seems all askew.

Airplanes land in his ears.

Birds nest in his beard.

If he seems askew to you,

Maybe it's your point of view.

Eyebrow Matters

Each Saturday morning
The neighbors all gather
To watch Harry Browzy
Work up a great lather.

The eyebrows he shaves
Keep up a quick pace.
First the left, then the right,
Grows straight down his face.

The eyebrows, themselves,
Show no sign of thinning,
Which suits Harry just fine,
As they are award winning.

Moose in Her Hair

Ruth put the wrong mousse in her hair.
Of course, the moose wanted to stay.
Though she combed and shampooed,
Rinsed and repeated,
The moose in her hair
Would not be defeated.

From then on, poor Ruth wore a hat
In an effort to hide her mistake.
For a moose in her hair,
Though it might entertain,
Was not something
She cared to explain!

Wiggly Piggly Kalamazoo

Blending in is hard to do
With a name like
Wiggly Piggly Kalamazoo.

Kalama-huh?
Kalama-what?
Kalama-who?

There are piles of Miles,
Scads of Brads,
Lots of Scotts,
Stacks of Jacks,
Gobs of Bobs,
Even scores of Theodores.

But what's a kid supposed to do
With a name like
Wiggly Piggly Kalamazoo?

Poodle On the Loose!

The McDougal's poodle escaped
Through a door left slightly ajar,
Jumped into the back of a taxi,
Which was the only available car.

The driver escorted the poodle
On a citywide sightseeing tour,
Pointing out any local attractions
That might appeal to the pooch.

When the cab returned the poodle,
The McDougals were waiting right there,
Happy to see their puppy,
Not so happy to pay the fare.

THUD!

Bud fell with a
THUD!
Into the mud
Wearing his Sunday suit.

To scrub off the
CRUD
He jumped into the tub
Wearing his Monday boots!

SOCK SKATING

I don't need a roller rink.
I skate beside the kitchen sink.
In socks that make me slip and slide,
Across the kitchen floor I glide!

I am a broom! I am a mop!
I pick up all the dust and slop!
If I had a few more pairs of feet,
The whole house would be just as neat!

Mission L.O.L.

Our humor-seeking rocket
Hurdled into space,
Blasting off in search
Of a fun and folly place,

A galaxy of giggles,
A silly solar system.
I felt like Galileo
On an exploration mission.

We went interplanetary
On our funny-finding flight,
And learned to laugh out loud
At the speed of light.

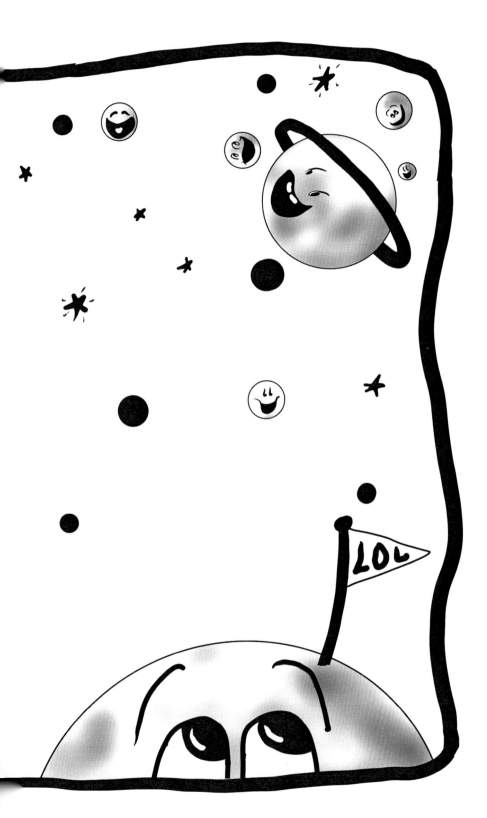

Oh, the Sounds You Can Make!

You can bark in the park,
Crow in the snow,
Squeak on a peak,
Cluck in a truck.

You can quack in a shack,
Growl in a towel,
Squawk in a frock,
Moo at the zoo.

But never,
Don't ever,

in a store!

The A-List Fish

Upon learning he'd made the list
Of the world's unattractive fish,
Blobfish wasn't much flattered
And avoided the chatter
Spreading through the sea.

Then from the crowd, a whisper,
"There he goes, the fish A-Lister!"
Which caused Blob to embrace
His unusual face
And his new notoriety.

The Very Unusual, Quite Peculiar, Completely Remarkable Day!

I stepped onto the curb
on Main Street.
There was no one
else in sight.
The sidewalk shifted
under my feet.
I was forced to sashay
to the right.

The first door I approached
stood ajar
To reveal what I
did not expect,
A hare cast out of a
barber's chair
By a button labeled,
"EJECT!"

I encountered a bull
in a china shop.
Cups and saucers
hit the floor.
A barista served
extra honey
To a tea-sipping
dinosaur.

Flamingos danced in
ballet shoes.
My head was
beginning to spin.
If I had to explain
the things I'd seen,
I wouldn't know
where to begin!

I retraced my steps
back to the place
Where things were
not so absurd.
And everything
was right again
When I stepped back
off the curb.

One Last Hat!

There was a commotion in Bonnetville
When the local hatmaker announced,
That make no mistake,
He had fabric to make
Just one last hat!

Since the beginning in Bonnetville,
Every man, woman, and child
Was required to wear,
Regardless of hair,
A hat like that.

As panic developed in Bonnetville,
The hatmaker came up with a plan
To cover the heads
Of all those in dread
With one last ...

**STUPENDOUS,
TREMENDOUS,**

**VOLUMIZED,
SUPERSIZED,**

**FANTASTIC,
ELASTIC**

HAT!

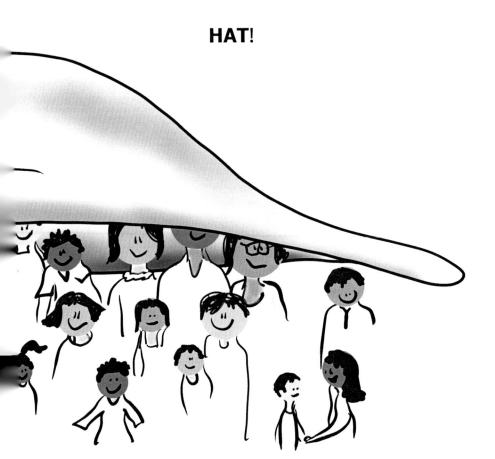

Piggy Bank

My piggy bank is a rattlesnake.
It doesn't have a snout.
It rattles when the tail shakes,
So the money

all

falls

out!

Marshmallow Hair

Grandma Joan has marshmallow hair.
It's fluffy, puffy, and white.
It's a cushion when she bumps her head,
A pillow to sleep on at night.

It doesn't move when the wind blows.
It barely fits through the door.
With hair like that, a kid like me
Wants to hug that grandma S'more!

Unicorn Disguise

Eleanore the unicorn
Hid her upside-down unihorn
Underneath a lampshade
That was plaid.

When Eleanore was asked
What the lampshade masked,
She told them all it was a
Trending fad.

But her secret was disclosed
When the bulb above her nose
Lit up when someone turned
On the lamp.

Lucy and Sue

Long-legged Lucy
And short-ankled Sue
Went pretty much
Everywhere together.

For Sue to keep up,
Lucy had to adjust
By facing forward
But walking backward.

A Different Kind of Pet

I don't want a dog.
I don't want a cat.
I don't want a pet
As simple as that.

A giraffe is too tall.
A dragon breathes fire.
A hippo's too mouthy.
A bird sits on a wire.

I don't want a horse.
I don't want a gnu.
A pig is too stinky.
What am I to do?

What pet do I want?
A pet I can ride.
A pet that won't eat much
And can come inside.

A pet that is funny.
A pet that is brave.
A pet I can sleep with,
But not in a cave!

I know what I want,
I know what kind of pet.
But my kind of pet
Isn't invented yet!

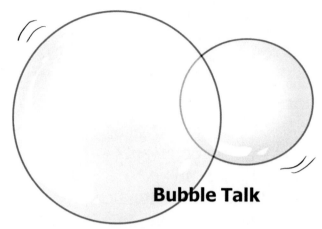

Bubble Talk

Bubbles come in all sizes
From really big to really small,
Depending on how hard you blow
Or if you breathe at all.

Sometimes they stick together
Or float up to the top.
But, in the end, they all say
The same thing ...

POP!

Dishwasher Love

I love our dishwasher.
It gets our
Dishes clean.

But, mostly, I love it
Because
It isn't me!

The Hunkerdowners

We are the Hunkerdowners.
We like to hunker down.
If there's a storm a-brewing,
You know where we'll be found.

We're not about to venture
Out on a raging sea.
Swirling snow and winds that blow
Are not our cup of tea.

PJ bottoms, cozy socks,
Cookies that are dunkers,
Are special treats for those of us
Who stay at home and hunker.

The Bank of Happy

When you deposit a smile,
A giggle, a snicker, a laugh,

Your Bank of Happy balance
Will grow on your behalf.

Diagnosis: Baloney!

"It looks like you're full of baloney,"
The doctor diagnosed,
After hearing the chuckle in my throat.

"There's a twinkle in your eye,
A bounce in your step,
But the symptoms I recognize the most

"Are rosy cheeks, dancing feet,
An overall delight,
All found during close examination.

"The cause of your condition
Is easy to conclude.
I'll give you a simple explanation.

"You're not full of baloney
From something that you ate,
It is, instead, from something that you read.

"The treatment I prescribe,
What will make you feel the best,
Is to read some baloney again!"

Made in United States
North Haven, CT
17 May 2024

52650499R00029